Key Takeaways & Analysis

of

General Stanley McChrystal's

Team of Teams

By Instaread

Please Note

This is key takeaways & analysis.

Table of Contents

OVERVIEW **4**

Important People..**7**

Key Takeaways...**10**

ANALYSIS **13**

Key Takeaway 1 ....**13**

Key Takeaway 2 ....**15**

Key Takeaway 3 ....**17**

Key Takeaway 4 ....**19**

Key Takeaway 5 ....**22**

Key Takeaway 6 ....**25**

Key Takeaway 7 ....**27**

Key Takeaway 8 ....**29**

Key Takeaway 9 ....**31**

Author's Style **34**

Perspective **36**

References **37**

OVERVIEW

Team of Teams by General Stanley McChrystal is an examination of the process he began of restructuring the Joint Special Operations Command management style, from a rigid command structure to a cooperative team comprised of smaller specialized teams. While fighting Al-Qaeda in Iraq (AQI), General McChrystal noted how the United States and coalition militaries were efficient war-fighting machines, but they were not adaptable or effective against the seemingly disordered AQI. In 2005, after a particularly destructive terrorist attack at the opening of a sewage plant near Baghdad, McChrystal began considering whether the efficient structure was actually hindering the counterinsurgency, preventing them from responding to threats in real time and delaying the capture of AQI leader Abu Musab al-Zarqawi.

Modern military management originated at the 1900 World's Fair, when Frederick Winslow Taylor revealed his work in steel production efficiency. Taylor believed that there is a right way to do any given thing, and he built reductionist processes to streamline how production employees work and what they need to know to do their jobs. In reductionist management schemes, employees focus only on their role and need not communicate with other employees or ask questions of their managers about the bigger picture.

Taylor's ideas reconfigured the world of work and entered soldiers' lives in the rigorous routines they must perform, their uniforms and supplies, and their inability to question their superiors or participate in decision-making processes. Lack of communication and involvement of the key operation participants in decision-making were identified as contributing factors in the failure to prevent the September 11, 2001 terrorist attacks on the World Trade Center towers in New York City and in the intelligence backlog between operators and analysts in Iraq.

Taking Navy SEAL training and successful team-building programs at Brigham and Women's Hospital in Boston and other organizations as his models, McChrystal describes the principles of building a team of teams with a common purpose, awareness, and empowerment in an environment where increased data availability and unpredictability arising from complexity seem to reward more hands-on command management styles.

Important People

General Stanley McChrystal: Stanley McChrystal was a four-star general in the United States Army, commander of the International Security Assistance Force, commander of the US Forces Afghanistan, and director of the Joint Staff. He wrote *Team of Teams* about his work to create a more adaptable, effective Joint Special Operations Command during the fight against Al-Qaeda in Iraq.

Tantum Collins: Tantum Collins is a graduate student and Marshall Scholar at the University of Cambridge. He took a course taught by McChrystal at Yale University as an undergraduate and participated in writing and researching *Team of Teams*.

David Silverman: David Silverman is the chief executive officer of CrossLead, a consultancy he co-founded with McChrystal. He was a US Navy SEAL officer, was deployed six times, and participated in writing and researching *Team of Teams*.

Chris Fussell: Chris Fussell is a partner at McChrystal's consultancy, CrossLead, formerly a

US Navy SEAL officer who served as an aide to McChrystal at the Joint Special Operations Command. Fussell participated in writing and researching *Team of Teams*.

Abu Musab al-Zarqawi: Abu Musab al-Zarqawi was the leader of Al-Qaeda in Iraq from 2004 until 2006, when he was killed in a bombing directed by McChrystal's Joint Special Operations Command.

Frederick Winslow Taylor: Frederick Winslow Taylor was a mechanical engineer who pioneered efficiency methods and data-driven scientific management during the early 1900s. His concepts became the worldwide standard in management for production.

Tarek al-Tayleb Mohamed Bouazizi: Mohamed Bouazizi was a fruit vendor in Tunisia who protested official corruption and harassment by self-immolating in public in 2010. The incident and subsequent protests of sympathetic activists set into motion the Tunisian Revolution and Arab Spring movements.

Admiral Horatio Nelson: Horatio Nelson was a flag officer of the British Royal Navy until his death in 1805. Nelson was known for his unconventional battle tactics.

George Mueller: George Mueller was the US National Aeronautics and Space Administration's associate administrator of the Office of Manned Space Flight in the 1960s as NASA worked toward the goal of a manned mission to the moon.

Michael Bloomberg: Michael Bloomberg is the founder and chief executive officer of financial data company Bloomberg LP, former mayor of New York City, and multi-billionaire. His bullpen management style is similar to that advocated by McChrystal.

Key Takeaways

1. An efficient system is not necessarily effective, especially if the output of the system is not what is needed or it does not make use of the inputs available. Creating an effective system can sometimes reduce its efficiency.

2. The reductionist approach to management revolutionized engineering and spread to other, non-production tasks. However, reductionist management does not work in every scenario.

3. Many processes in the world today are more complex than they were before the information age, making them highly unpredictable and making a reductionist management style less effective. Reduction is still effective in complicated systems, which are more predictable than complex ones.

4. A robust system is effective at countering a specific obstacle, but a resilient system can adapt to unexpected obstacles. A robust system can be fragile if it is not also resilient, and making a resilient system may mean reducing the system's efficiency at

countering the threat against which it was designed.

5. A team needs a sense of purpose and trust between members above all to successfully accomplish more than a single person could alone.

6. Creating successful teams can still result in difficulties if different teams do not trust each other. A team of teams consists of cohesive, specialized groups that trust each other to do their jobs and communicate throughout a task.

7. The physical layout of working space can encourage or discourage collaboration and communication. Cubicles and individual offices encourage isolation and territoriality, while open floor plans allow employees to see each other, talk casually, and trust one another.

8. Organization members that do not trust each other do not share information and resent sharing limited resources. Members of teams that trust each other share information and willingly give up access to resources when they know it will benefit the organization's common purpose.

9. The role of a leader in a team of teams is more similar to that of a gardener than the traditional self-confident, omnipotent commander. Leaders who resist the urge to monitor and instruct, and who leave decisions to those further down the chain of command, get equally good decisions and a more efficient organization.

ANALYSIS

Key Takeaway 1

An efficient system is not necessarily effective, especially if the output of the system is not what is needed or it does not make use of the inputs available. Creating an effective system can sometimes reduce its efficiency.

Analysis

It seems that a manager's goal should be to create an effective system first, and that efficiency will follow with time to tweak the processes or find motivated employees. However, legacy systems adapted to a new situation or repurposed for a new output may still seek efficiency even as it loses effectiveness. When a system designed to take in pizza ingredients and produce pizzas is altered to take in pie ingredients and produce pies, retaining processes that made good pizzas, but reduces the quality of pies, or it can overlook opportunities for increased quality or efficiency in pie-making, even if the system produces pie just as quickly as it produced pizza.

Armies of the world have discovered that, with the rise of non-state actors, war today does not resemble the state-driven wars of the past where leaders relied on the support of their citizens and utilized treaties and negotiations. However, the modern army still relies on processes developed prior to the counterinsurgency focus. Just as snipers revolutionized the battlefield during the US Revolutionary War, because no one had considered hiding soldiers in trees rather than lining them up in ranks, war innovators have a considerable advantage over their opponents. The other side is burdened with searching for a solution to the new ideas and also slowly developing their own innovations.

Key Takeaway 2

The reductionist approach to management revolutionized engineering and spread to other, non-production tasks. However, reductionist management does not work in every scenario.

Analysis

Reductionist management is best suited to tasks that must be completed repeatedly, the same way every time, as quickly as possible. Any job that can be reduced to a list of instructions is well-suited to this management style, where workers are not expected to communicate with their colleagues, form a team, or ask questions of their supervisors. For example, on a factory assembly line there is no need for a worker to think of every door installed on a car differently. Uniformity is valued over creativity. Efficiency is the primary goal because the instructions ensure that the process is effective, taking the appropriate inputs, and generating the appropriate outputs. A task, like putting a door on a car, could possibly be done by a robot given the same list of instructions. However, sometimes humans cannot be replaced by robots on the factory floor because of limitations in the design of robots.

By comparison, there are many jobs that cannot be reduced to a set of instructions, and no one would want them managed in a reductionist way, such as doctors and lawyers. For them, efficiency means nothing if a doctor is not effective. While a lawyer may have a set procedure for every court case, starting with meeting the client and moving on to which motions to file in court, that procedure does not resemble a reductionist instruction list. A doctor who treated every patient identically or a lawyer who treated every case identically would not be effective because what their jobs really entail is creativity and adaptive thinking. They need a holistic view of the case at hand to make those decisions, and would not be effective if their knowledge in the field is so narrow as to leave them oblivious if a case does not go as planned.

Key Takeaway 3

Many processes in the world today are more complex than they were before the information age, making them highly unpredictable and making a reductionist management style less effective. Reduction is still effective in complicated systems, which are more predictable than complex ones.

Analysis

The difference between a complicated system and a complex one is the difference between a car and ocean currents. In theory, a car should work if all the parts are in working order, and failure of one part, like a fuse, has a predictable effect on the car, like the interior lights failing. Diagnosing a car can be difficult because the systems are interconnected and some parts are difficult to see, but the range of inputs that impact its functioning are limited, and the outputs are predictable.

On the other hand, ocean currents take a knowable set of inputs and their output motions can be predicted, but the range of inputs is so large as to be unmeasurable, making prediction of the output less reliable. Ocean currents can be so complex that, in one circumstance, the path of a herd of whales may change the direction or force of a current and, in another, the same pod of whales will change nothing substantially. As McChrystal points out, a butterfly flapping its wings may cause a hurricane on the other side of the world, but it is known from observation that it does not happen every time a butterfly flaps its wings.

Aside from the difficulty of diagnosing a problem in a car, the process of fixing one is reductionist in nature. A mechanic could be very effective and efficient if they replace every fuse in a given make, model, and year of car the same way. If replacing a fuse does not solve the problem, it would be because the inputs were not accurately assessed and some other system, like the car's dome light, is faulty. And then the mechanic could not go wrong replacing every dome light in a given type of car the same way. A complicated system is predictable because it shows linear results. However, a complex system shows non-linear results. Too many things can impact a complex system for reasons that are often too complicated to understand, such as a butterfly that can cause a hurricane simply by beating its wings. These linear and non-linear results are the difference between complex and complicated systems.

Key Takeaway 4

A robust system is effective at countering a specific obstacle, but a resilient system can adapt to unexpected obstacles. A robust system can be fragile if it is not also resilient, and making a resilient system may mean reducing the system's efficiency at countering the threat against which it was designed.

Analysis

Highly specialized solutions to problems often arise in response to a significant tragedy, described as the never again mentality. And, in some cases, these robust systems are completely necessary, even if they are not resilient. Car airbags are a robust system because they deploy in response to a specific event and generally do their job, which is to inflate rapidly and prevent passengers from being hurt by impact with the car's interior. However, airbags are not resilient. They only inflate where they are placed, do not prevent other types of injury, like whiplash, and sometimes they inflate when a collision has not occurred. Just because airbags are a fragile, robust system does not mean cars should not be made with them. They still save more lives than they take, and removing them would expose people to much greater danger.

No car maker has created a truly resilient collision safety system, but newer cars do come with more resilient systems that better protect passengers or can prevent accidents entirely. These are created by systems working in tandem, starting with more airbags, crumple zones, stronger frames, shatter-proof glass, and seat belts, and in newer cars incorporating rear-view cameras, proximity sensors, and automatic braking for crash avoidance. Cars are not likely to be able to repair themselves or their passengers in the future, so adaptive crash prevention systems come close to as resilient as car safety systems can get.

If a car were designed to prevent only one type of accident, like skidding off the road due to snow, it might have features like permanent snow chains on the tires. However, that would make the car less effective in nearly every other scenario and, in an accident during different weather, those features could cause more damage than if those features were not there. Another example would be the Netherlands' reaction to a flood that happened in 1958. The Rhine River flooded, killing 1,800 people. To prevent a similar disaster, the country constructed the Delta Works, flood walls meant to hold back a new flood. However, flooding again hit the area in 1993 and 1995, but it came from snow melting off the Alps. The flood walls prevented the water from draining. This example shows that some robust systems cause more harm than good when faced with situations other than the one for which they were designed. Reducing the car's efficiency of crash prevention in snow, by making snow chains removable, increases its effective safety in other scenarios.

Key Takeaway 5

A team needs a sense of purpose and trust between members above all to successfully accomplish more than a single person could alone.

Analysis

Team-building has been an organizational concept for a long time already, but in some organizations the message of teamwork is undermined by a message of competition or by a lack of support from supervisors. Common purpose for team members relies on consistent focus on the goal of the team, not of the individual, and many organizations fail to recognize the contradiction when they send groups to team-building seminars and also give incentives to individuals for achieving more than their team members. Wherever the competitive, individual-focused initiative is added, teams break down.

Similarly, organizations that encourage teams to make decisions may also allow the team supervisor to separate themselves from their decision-making process, give the supervisor decisions to make without input from the team, or restrict the information that the supervisor can give to the team. An example of the detriment of giving one person ultimate decision making power over everyone else is the crash of United Airlines Flight 173. In 1978, Flight 173 had landing gear problems. The pilot was warned multiple times by his crew members that fuel was running dangerously low. However, the pilot ignored these warnings, choosing to wait until the ground crew was prepared for their landing. As a result, the pilot allowed the plane to run out of fuel and it crashed. A flight crew must work as a team. Instead, this captain failed to listen to his fellow teammates, possibly believing that it was more important to dictate everyone else's actions and make major decisions on his own.

Creating a team that demonstrates trust and a common sense of purpose is not a reductionist process, and proving that the team has these qualities may not be possible in some cases. Perseverance is demonstrated by the soldiers in the US Navy SEAL training program, Basic Underwater Demolition SEALS training (BUD/S), a six month program required of all aspiring SEALS. This program is one indicator of a successful team because they understand the need to rely on each other to accomplish the goal, and not relying on the team out of pride results in failure for the whole team.

Key Takeaway 6

Creating successful teams can still result in difficulties if different teams do not trust each other. A team of teams consists of cohesive, specialized groups that trust each other to do their jobs and communicate throughout a task.

Analysis

Teams are often restricted in size to ensure maximum trust and strong relationships between members because the human brain is only capable of trusting a limited number of people. This was probably a useful feature in human evolution, where tribes could move more quickly if they were smaller and were better served by defaulting to distrust of other tribes. In large organizations, tribalism appears again when different regional sales teams engage in competition without a management incentive to compete, or when a team of designers displays lack of confidence in the engineers responsible for making their plans viable. Sometimes this insulation happens because organizations do not encourage communication between these separate teams. Once a design is sent to the engineers, the architects do not get to see how the engineers work to implement the designs. Instead, architects are expected to move on to designing the next project and not distract themselves with something outside of their job descriptions.

The European efforts to join the space race are especially demonstrative because the different countries' engineering teams felt an incentive to keep secrets from each other, and that cooperation was a liability. These ideas were motivated by a patriotic feeling as well as economic advantages.

Key Takeaway 7

The physical layout of working space can encourage or discourage collaboration and communication. Cubicles and individual offices encourage isolation and territoriality, while open floor plans allow employees to see each other, talk casually, and trust one another.

Analysis

Open floor plans are a significant trend in startup culture and in any company looking to adapt quickly like a startup. Even small, one- or two-person operations see the benefit of being around peers and having people available for casual conversations, which is one reason coworking spaces have sprung up in a variety of cities. At these spaces, small organizations can rent a desk or cubicle and share resources like printers, kitchens, and lounges. Sometimes coworking spaces will offer interest clubs or recreational sports to encourage connections between renters.

The open floor plan and mobility of work space has served video game company Valve Software well. They recently published their handbook for new employees to share some of their insights into how best to develop strong team workspaces. [1] Valve employees work at rolling desks, and there are outlets available throughout the office rooms, so employees can simply unplug, roll to a new location, and plug in there whenever they need a change. Teams generally roll their desks together to facilitate communication, but the handbook also encourages new employees looking for interesting projects to roll their desks over next to someone they would like to work with or whose work they admire.

The notion that in-person communication is necessary for problem-solving also gained attention when Marissa Mayer eliminated the option to work from home after she became CEO of the media company Yahoo. Many people criticized her for making the corporate culture less friendly to parents, Mayer being a new parent herself, but management experts found her policy change encouraged "serendipitous interaction" between employees, strengthening connections face to face that could not be developed long-distance and encouraging employees to toss ideas around for longer periods of time.[2]

Key Takeaway 8

Organization members that do not trust each other do not share information and resent sharing limited resources. Members of teams that trust each other share information and willingly give up access to resources when they know it will benefit the organization's common purpose.

Analysis

In a command of teams where teams do not collaborate and their leaders still fit into a rigid command structure, those teams engage in tribalistic distrust of one another and naturally resent when their access to a valuable resource, like vehicles, is restricted in favor of another team. Not being involved in the decision of where the resource would be best put to use, teams would view this resource reassignment as favoritism and have no way of knowing whether the resource was really put to its best possible use. One of the most surprising revelations McChrystal had while reorganizing the Joint Special Operations Command was that when teams were involved in the decision to assign important resources, how the resources were used, and how those resources were beneficial, they were more willing to volunteer to give up resources to other teams. They did so on the assumption that when they needed the resource, the other teams would be willing to give up their own access in return.

In war, information is power, and the natural inclination of leaders is to restrict access to that information as much as possible to prevent a leak. Secrecy cannot be compromised by teamwork because troop movements and limitations are too valuable in enemy hands. But there is value in informing more than just the upper ranks about operations because contextual information about intelligence and about every step of the operation benefits the people charged with making decisions at every level of the war effort.

Key Takeaway 9

The role of a leader in a team of teams is more similar to that of a gardener than the traditional self-confident, omnipotent commander. Leaders who resist the urge to monitor and instruct, and who leave decisions to those further down the chain of command, get equally good decisions and a more efficient organization.

Analysis

Today, it is not uncommon for employees in a company to copy their supervisors on all emails, wear badges that track their movements around offices, and consent to having their computers monitored for internet access, generating enormous volumes of data that are analyzed for efficiency and adherence to company policies. With radio frequency identification, near-field communication, network surveillance, and data analysis technology growing in capability, employers see their opportunities to manage employees more thoroughly than ever before. However, McChrystal urges leaders to do the opposite. He encourages them to watch and communicate, but only intervene when absolutely necessary and allow workers to make decisions without having to get approval all the way up the chain of command.

His guidance is linked to the strength of surveillance technology and communication today. Where previously soldiers conducting reconnaissance hunted for their target on foot for days and struggled to receive updated intelligence or communicate their questions back to analysts, drone surveillance allows an analyst to keep eyes on an operation from beginning to end, follow a target for weeks at a time, get high-resolution, current images to identify the target in person, and see exactly who the operators are apprehending, or whether they are chasing the wrong vehicle. In these cases, it does little good to ask a general whether to apprehend a target. If the leadership has already instructed soldiers to apprehend someone, the drone pilot and analyst have identified them, and the operators clearly have the right person in their sights, the team can quickly determine how best to apprehend the target in the moment, rather than waking up the general for approval.

Just as a gardener chooses the best plant varieties for the soil, sunlight, and water conditions in a part of the garden, leaders' responsibilities can be more managerial than instructive when all they have to do is remove obstacles (weeds and pests) and provide motivation (fertilizer). In doing so, the leader is really cultivating more capable leaders by distributing responsibilities as they are best suited.

Author's Style

Team of Teams is written in the style of a lecture, starting with an anecdote and expanding into the factors that contributed to the anecdote, then the problems presented by the incident, the sources of those problems, and the solution. The narrative winds this way through various historical examples and more recent relevant events. Readers get a front-row view of the fight against AQI inside the Joint Special Operations Command, following McChrystal's decision-making process. McChrystal also describes his personal influences, the people he has worked with, and failed operations alongside successful ones. The descriptions of historical examples, the response of Brigham and Women's Hospital surgical teams, the Boston Marathon Bombings, and the crash of Flight 137, are thorough, well-cited, and descriptive. Overall, the text provides a balance of the advantages of some systems and their drawbacks. There is not much jargon in the text, and any military-specific terms are defined the first time they are used.

Dialogue is easy to follow even when it happened between military officials regarding their operations, which is surprising considering their use of acronyms. The text also includes diagrams that demonstrate McChrystal's messages about organization.

Each of the various chapters highlights either a managerial problem facing McChrystal and the Joint Special Operations Command in Iraq, or an ideal of leadership and teamwork that contributes to the successful operation of teams of teams. The chapters also follow the command's progress toward the new management scheme chronologically, so they flow into each other without jarring transitions. Since the focus is on the system's failures at the beginning and its successes at the end, the reader sees the gradual process of change and improvement with a neat resolution.

Perspective

Stanley Allen McChrystal is a retired US Army general. McChrystal was Commander of the International Security Assistance Force, commander of the US Forces Afghanistan, and as Director of the Joint Staff. In his new position as a consultant, McChrystal works with companies to implement management structures similar to the one he developed at the Joint Special Operations Command.

~~~~~~~ END OF INSTAREAD~~~~~~~

References

1. Valve: Handbook for New Employees, March 2012, http://www.valvesoftware.com/company/Valve_Handbook_LowRes.pdf

2. Henn, Steve. "'Serendipitous Interaction Key To Tech Firms' Workplace Design," National Public Radio. 13 March 2013, http://www.npr.org/sections/alltechconsidered/2013/03/13/174195695/serendipitous-interaction-key-to-tech-firms-workplace-design

CPSIA information can be obtained at www.ICGtesting.com
Printed in the USA
LVOW04s0851181015

458736LV00020B/474/P